MONTANA

A Turner Educational Services, Inc. book. Based on the Portrait of America television series created by R.E. (Ted) Turner.

Library of Congress Number: 87-26465

Library of Congress Cataloging in Publication Data

Thompson, Kathleen.
    Montana.

    (Portrait of America)
    "A Turner book."
    Summary: Discusses the history, economy, culture, and future of Montana. Also includes a state chronology, pertinent statistics, and maps.
    1. Montana—Juvenile literature. [1. Montana] I. Title. II. Series: Thompson, Kathleen. Portrait of America.
    F731.3.T48   1987   978.6—dc19   87-26465

ISBN 0-8174-468-0   hardcover library binding

ISBN 0-8114-6792-9   softcover binding

Cover Photo: Jack Olson

    4 5 6 7 8 9 0   96 95 94 93 92 91

★ ★ ★ ★ ★

Portrait of AMERICA

MONTANA

Kathleen Thompson

STECK-VAUGHN
C O M P A N Y
A Subsidiary of National Education Corporation

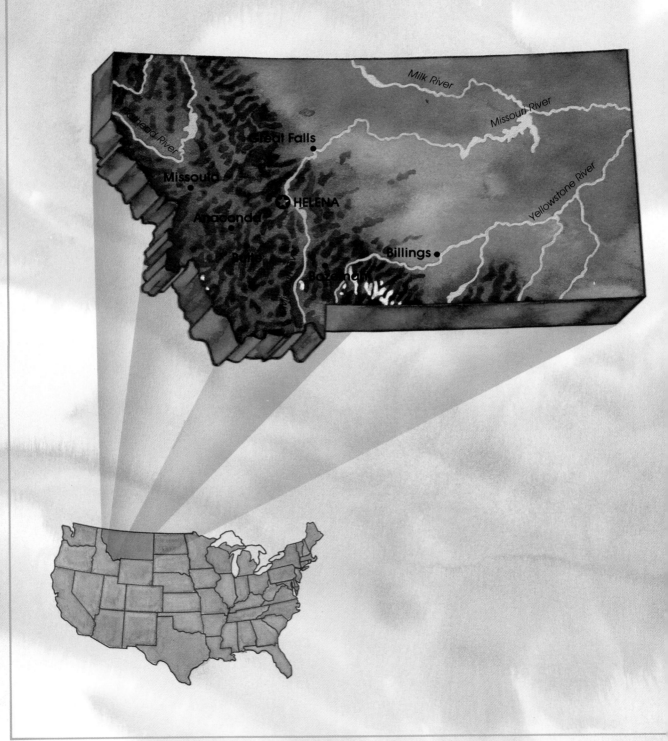

CONTENTS

Introduction

Montana, the Treasure State.

"I love it because it's so deep. In the eastern states, you can hit the sky with a rifle bullet. You can't do it here."

Montana: mountains, minerals, cattle, coal, and copper.

"Montana is our home. It has been here a long time, and we have been here a long time. And it doesn't make any difference when you come here. It belongs to all of us."

Some places you look around and everywhere you see what humanity has done—fields planted in rows, farms, factories, cities. In Montana, people have left their mark only in scattered patches on a vast, magnificent world of nature. Here life is lived with a strong sense of closeness to the land . . . and the things in it are still free.

The Ancient Land

Ten thousand years ago, there were Indians living on the land we call Montana. When the first white men came to this land, they found expert riders who sat straight and tall on their horses. The Blackfeet, Assiniboine, Crow, Cheyenne, and Gros Ventre lived east of the Rockies, the Shoshone to the southwest. They hunted buffalo for food and for hides to make their tents and clothing. In the western moutains lived the Kutenai, Kalispel, and Flathead, who hunted deer and fished in the clear streams.

Before any European had stood on the earth of Montana, France had claimed it. France, in 1682, claimed all of the land which drained into the Mississippi River. That land then went to Spain, back to France, and finally to the United States,

An 1882 photo of a Cheyenne Indian girl.

in the Louisiana Purchase of 1803. It was now a quarter of a century after the American Revolution and the Montana Indians had seen only a few white fur traders on their land.

The year after President Thomas Jefferson bought the Lousiana Territory from France, he sent an expedition out to explore it. The group was headed by Meriwether Lewis and William Clark. It was guided by Sacagawea, a Shoshone woman.

Lewis and Clark reached Montana in 1805. They explored the area and went on toward the Pacific, their final goal. But from that time on, other white men came to Montana and did not leave.

The first wave of non-Indians

such as the Canadian North West Company, and later, the Hudson's Bay Company.

These traders made friends with the people of Montana. They did not try to take the land away from the Indians. They brought in goods that the Indians could not yet make for themselves. For a short time, Indians and whites lived in peace in Montana. During this time, the fur traders explored the country, making maps.

Everything changed in July of 1862. The place was called Grasshopper Creek. What happened there was the discovery of gold.

As far back as 1852, a man named Finlay found gold in the lower Deer Lodge Valley. And six years after that, James and Granville Stuart found more at Gold Creek. Then, in 1860, a road was built from Ft. Benton to Ft. Walla Walla. A few prospectors started looking further afield. What they found, first at Grasshopper Creek, then at Alder Gulch, Last Chance

onto Indian land was made up of fur traders. There was Manuel Lisa's Missouri Fur Company. Lisa built the first trading post in Montana on the Bighorn River in 1807. There was the Rocky Mountain Fur Company. It came up into Montana from the south. There were the American Fur Company, owned by John Jacob Astor, and British fur companies

11

Gulch, and Confederate Gulch, were some of the richest placer deposits in the world.

The rush was on.

Between July of 1862 and winter of that same year, thousands of prospectors had poured into the area. The town of Bannack had sprung up almost overnight. The next year, at Alder Gulch, Virginia City was born. Soon there were boom towns all over the area. There was also trouble.

With so much gold and so little government, there were bound to be outlaws. The worst of them was the Henry Plummer gang. They operated around the Bannack-Virginia City area. To deal with the Plummer gang, a group called the Vigilantes of Montana was formed. The vigilantes broke up the gang, but it was clear that Montana needed some kind of

The lodge of Indian leader Two Moons (below) was photographed at Lame Deer, Montana, in 1896.

Coffrin's Old West Gallery Inc.

government, especially when mining strikes led to violence. So, in 1864, the Territory of Montana was formed and a governor was appointed.

While outlaws were bringing terror to the settlers, the settlers were bringing terror to the Indians. Whites moved onto land that had belonged to the Indians for thousands of years. They slaughtered the buffalo and deer that were the core of the Indian way of life. They forced the Indians onto ever smaller and more distant bits of land. They made treaties that allowed the Indians to remain on parts of their land and then, when the whites decided that that land might be valuable, they broke the treaties.

Many of the Montana tribes refused to fight. They settled peacefully on one reservation after another. But there were others who would not give up. They attacked wagon trains and settlements. They stole cattle and horses from the settlers.

After the Civil War, U.S. military forces were brought in to deal with the Indians. Battles were fought between the Sioux and Cheyenne and the U.S. troops

Gravemarkers at the site of Custer's Last Stand.

until 1876. In that year, Dull Knife, Sitting Bull, Crazy Horse and Two Moons defeated Lt. Colonel George Custer at the Battle of the Little Bighorn.

The Indians had won the battle, but they had lost the war. The United States took revenge for the deaths of Custer and his men by bringing overwhelming military force against the Indians. In 1877, major Indian resistance to the white takeover of their land ended. Chief Joseph led the Nez Percé through Montana during their retreat from Idaho, toward their final defeat in the Bear Paw Mountains.

The two cultures: this 1882 photo shows a tepee pitched alongside the railroad track.

It was not primarily the prospectors who forced the Indians off their land. It was the cattlemen. Cattle had first been brought into Montana to feed the miners. Then, in the 1870s large herds were brought up from from Texas to graze on Montana's open range. The Northern Pacific Railroad reached the area in 1883, giving the ranchers easy transportation for their cattle to the faraway markets.

Ranchers did very well in Montana until the winter of 1886. Then terrible weather killed huge numbers of cattle. Many smaller ranchers went out of business completely. Those who remained had to start growing winter feed and the open range was divided up.

In 1884, Montana had applied for statehood, but the Congress said no. The territory had a constitution and there was every reason to admit it to the Union. At that time, however, Congress was evenly divided politically and no one wanted to rock the boat. Five years later, Montana and three other western territo-

At right, the first Cat Creek oil well.

ries were all given statehood. Montana became the 41st state in 1889.

Things did not calm down much in Montana after it became a state. For one thing, there was the "war of the copper kings."

While mining had remained big in Montana, gold had been replaced by silver and silver by copper. The biggest copper miners were William A. Clark and Marcus Daly and later, F. Augustus Heinze.

During the 1890s Daly and Clark fought for power in the state. They bought up newspapers. They tried to bribe state legislators. Daly claimed that Clark had bought his way into the U.S. Senate and Clark was not allowed to take his seat.

Just before his death in 1900, Daly sold his Anaconda Copper Company to Standard Oil. Standard Oil already had large investments in lumber and other Montana industry. With control of Anaconda-Amalgamated, Standard Oil gained tremendous power in Montana.

Montana Historical Society

15

But the third copper king entered the field now. F. Augustus Heinze started fighting for political and economic control and he used a powerful weapon. He had friends among Montana's judges. These judges ruled that Heinze could mine ore from lands next door to his own. A lot of that land belonged to Amalgamated. And Amalgamated didn't take it lying down.

The battles between Heinze and Amalgamated made Montana a colorful and sometimes dangerous place to live for the next few years. Finally, in 1903, Amalgamated suddenly shut down all its mines. This convinced the governor and the legislature that they had to do something about the situation. They passed a law that robbed Heinze of his power through the judges. The mines reopened and, in 1906, Heinze sold out to Amalgamated.

Montana was now a one company state. By 1915, the Montana economy revolved around copper. The copper industry affected Montana politics. It even owned a chain of local newspapers until 1959.

Agriculture, other than cattle-raising, came slowly to Montana. The state was hard to reach and much of the land was dry. But early in the twentieth century, the railroads started advertising in Europe and in the eastern United States for homesteaders. And in 1909, Congress passed the Enlarged Homestead Act.

For several years, homestead-

ers poured into Montana by the thousands. When World War I brought high wheat prices, there was an even larger rush of farmers into the state. Montana was in a farming boom that was like the mining boom of the 1860s. But it didn't last. Starting in 1918, there was a series of droughts. The war ended and wheat prices went down. The boom had gone bust. Montana agriculture did not completely recover until World War II.

In the meantime, oil was discovered. During the 1920s a number of oil refineries were built in the state but it wasn't until the great Williston Basin oil-

Below: A nineteenth century farmer uses a horse-drawn plow.

Montana Historical Society

Montana Travel Promotion

fields were opened in 1951 that oil became Montana's leading mineral.

Like the rest of the country, Montana suffered greatly from the droughts of the same years. Mines closed. The lumber industry all but shut down. Farm harvests dried in the fields. But the federal government started huge programs for irrigating the land, conserving the soil, bringing electricity to farm areas, and controlling destructive insects.

18

And World War II brought a tremendous demand for Montana's minerals.

For a long time, Montana's politics continued to be linked with the big mining companies. The Republican and Democratic parties had been just about equally powerful and, up until World War II, the political campaigns were often between the large corporations and their opponents.

Montana gave women the right to vote in 1914. In 1916, Montana elected Jeannette Rankin to the U.S. House of Representatives. She was the first woman to be elected to the U.S. Congress. It was not until three years later that the Nineteenth Amendment to the U.S. Constitution was passed guaranteeing the right to vote to women all over the country.

In 1972, Montana adopted a new constitution. It showed clearly what the people of Montana had come to feel was important. It emphasized the need for a clean and healthful environment. It prohibited corporations and individuals from discrimination on the basis of race. And it stated that one of the goals of the state was to preserve the cultures of Montana's Indians.

Left-hand page: Jeannette Rankin is pictured against a scenic view of Flathead Lake. At right, a Sioux warrior's grave. The closing of the frontier ended a way of life for the Plains Tribes.

19

Ken Ryan and four prior tribal chairmen celebrate the 1987 Fort Peck Assiniboine and Sioux Centennial.

The sign in the photo reads:

TRIBAL CHAIRMEN
PRESENT- KENNY RYAN
FORMER
NORMAN HOLLOW
JOE RED THUNDER
BILL YOUPEE
PETE EAGLE

New Life

"Historically, in the past, when the buffalo herds fattened, when the migratory fowl came back, when the prairies turned green, that was a signal to our people from the Creator that this was a new year. The pow-wow is a celebration of life, a new year's celebration, if you will. (We celebrate) that yes, we have made it through another hard winter, and we are here in the springtime. We give thanks to the Creator that we are going to live another year."

Kenneth Ryan is chairman of Montana's Assiniboine and Sioux tribes. And these days, those tribes have a lot to celebrate. That was not always the case, of course. In the past, Montana's native Americans suffered indignity, injustice, and death at the hands of the white man.

"It would be to our benefit to always remember what has happened to us. And we can all work to make sure that

Right: a fancy dance competition features a colorful display of traditional tribal costumes.

21

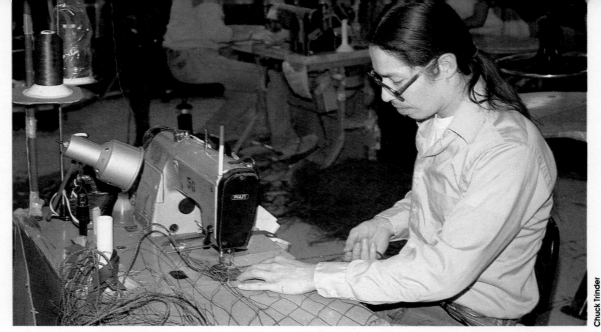

A & S Tribal Industries makes products for the armed forces. Above, a worker sewing camouflage netting.

something like this never happens again, to any race of people. But nevertheless, bitterness is an emotion which serves no purpose."

The greatest wrong done to native Americans was that they were forced off their lands onto reservations. The reservations were always land that seemed worthless to the white man. In Montana, the land that makes up its seven reservations has turned out to be far from worthless. It contains oil, coal, and natural gas.

At left, Fort Peck Tribal Executive Board members, members of the A & S Oil and Gas Department, and drill operators pose with the "Winona" oil well.

The tribes that Kenneth Ryan leads have financed and drilled their own oil well. They have also created a company called A & S Industries where members of the tribe work to fill defense contracts for the very army that once forced them off their land.

The Assiniboine and Sioux tribe members have made a new beginning in the land of their ancestors. While they hold to the traditions of the past, they have shown that they can mold their own future.

"It is the only way to go, to be self-reliant, because it means you are captain of your own destiny."

23

Earl and Sylvia Duvall are pictured above.

Bald-Headed Prairie

"To me it was a bald-headed prairie and it was heartless. It didn't have a schoolhouse, it didn't have any roads. The poor livestock didn't have any trees to stand under. I just couldn't get over it. I wouldn't marry a farmer and live on this bald-headed prairie. No, sir! I was gonna go someplace. Add I did. I didn't stay long. I came back."

Sylvia Duvall was only six years old when she first stood and looked at the bald-headed prairie. The years that followed didn't make her think a lot more kindly about Montana.

First, her family lived in a shack that was no more than eight feet by ten feet—smaller than the average bedroom.

"There was just barely enough room to set a chair. The bed hung on the wall on hinges and at night you would put it down to go to bed."

Still, the land was rich and the crops were good. For awhile. Then . . .

"One year we were hailed out. Next year we were hopped out—by the grasshoppers. And the third year we was blowed out, and I mean blowed out! The dirt was so high in fence lines and stuff, around buildings! And driving, the horses'd get out of breath and choke. They'd just get on their knees and cough."

Things got so bad during the years of the wind storms that Sylvia once went over a whole forty acres to get enough feed to fill one washtub. Most of the neighbors had to give up and leave.

"We had kind of a farewell party for the last two families that were there. And when I got home, I just couldn't go to sleep. I sat on the porch and cried."

In this 1929 photo, Sylvia and Earl are shown with their first automobile.

In the end, Sylvia married a farmer and lived to see her children and grandchildren take over the farm. And she has to admit that she grew to love that old bald-headed prairie.

"I have no regrets. I wish I could *live it over again. Even to come out to that homestead shack. I wouldn't set and pout and cry because I didn't have my own bedroom. Yes, I think it's been a very good life. I can't see a life anywhere else that'd have been as good and as free."*

25

Riches Out of the Land

In the days when the copper kings battled it out for control of the state, Montana's economy depended almost entirely on this one reddish metal. When Augustus Heinze sold out to Anaconda-Amalgamated, the economy depended on one company. But things have changed.

The change started in the 1940s and it was caused by three things: tourists, defense spending, and oil.

It's easy to see why tourists would be drawn to Montana. It's an awesomely beautiful state with a colorful history, filled with cowboys and gold mines and desperados. It's a place that hasn't been spoiled much by progress and the industrial revolution. Tourists are one reason that about three quarters of the state's income comes from services—restaurants,

Montana coal mines produce more than thirty-two million tons of coal each year.

David Hiser / Big Sky Resort

Above, skiing at Big Sky. Malmstrom Air Force Base (at right and below) is a major employer in this state.

shops, laundries, hotels, physicians, that sort of thing.

"Services" also includes government. In Montana, government is the second largest employer in the state. Many of those employed by the federal government work at Malmstrom Air Force Base near Great Falls or at missile sites in northern Montana. The defense spending that started during World War II has continued through the following decades. It has contributed greatly to Montana's prosperity.

Of course, Montana could suffer a slump in her economy if defense spending is ever cut back.

Finally, there is oil. The first

MHF photos

28

Montana Power Company

Michael Reagan

Yellowstone Raft Co.

Left: an open pit coal mine. Montana rivers draw fishermen (below) and rafting enthusiasts (above).

drilling for oil started in 1915, but it was 1951 when the great Williston Basin fields opened. Those fields made oil Montana's most important mineral.

The trio of tourists, missiles, and oil broke forever the hold that copper had on Montana. Now, the state is still a leading copper producer, but coal is its second most important mineral.

Manufacturing in Montana consists mostly of processing its natural resources. The two leading industries are wood products and food processing. Montana has about a hundred sawmills. And factories around the state refine sugar and mill flour. Other plants process the ore from Montana mines.

29

Montana agriculture has had its ups and downs. The land was not used for farming until the twentieth century. A very promising farming boom was cut short by droughts. Then agriculture bounced back during World War II.

Today, the largest part of Montana's farmland is used for grazing livestock—beef and dairy cattle and sheep. Livestock products account for about half of all farm income.

Montana's field crops include wheat and barley, hay, potatoes, and sugar beets. Much of the farmland in the state is irrigated.

Oh, yes, one more thing. Montana grows three million Christmas trees a year. That's a lot of holiday cheer for one state.

On the left-hand page: Rocky Mountain Log Homes turns timber into beautiful modern-day "log cabins."

Above is a farm near Adler. Below: livestock account for half of Montana farm income.

Jolene Langin Baldwin is pictured above.

One Room, One Teacher

"My mother really thinks it's neat. But my father thinks I'm a little crazy for being out here. And my sisters— one thinks it's okay and the other thinks I'm real brave but she wouldn't do it for anything."

Jolene Langin Baldwin teaches in a special kind of school. Most people probably think that this kind of school doesn't exist anymore. But in Montana, it has to.

Jolene teaches in a one-room school. All the students, no matter what grade they're in, sit in the same classroom. And Jolene teaches them all. She also lives fifty miles from the nearest town—and eighty miles from her friend Michelle Mansanti, who teaches in another one-room school.

"You're everything at the school— curriculum director, science teacher, art teacher, P.E. teacher, janitor, principal. The only thing you're not is a superintendent. And a parent."

When Michelle gets home from school, she sometimes reaches for the phone and calls another friend, Sherri Oster, who teaches in *another* one-room school.

Right: Jolene is shown with her pupils. Students in different grades share one classroom.

ALL VISITORS
MUST REPORT
TO OFFICE

33

"I was brought up in a stern type atmosphere with teachers where they were just out of my reach. But these children look at me as someone they can talk to and if they have a problem, they ask me."

You have to like teaching a lot to be willing to live out in the middle of nowhere and deal with the problems of a one-room school. But it has its good side too.

"Some days it's really frustrating. You just want to scream because it's six subjects and seven grades. But other days it's fun because you don't get bored."

With teachers like Jolene Langin Baldwin, Michelle Mansanti, and Sherri Oster, it's a pretty safe bet that the students don't get bored either.

At left, Sherri Oster helps out a young pupil.
Right-hand page: Sherri, Jolene, and Michelle.

Art West

It would be difficult to say which is more striking—Montana's extraordinary landscape or its colorful history. Here the mountains soar, the plains roll, the sky stretches out forever. And traced on the air are images of cowboys riding hard at roundup, Indians ranging the hills on the bare backs of their horses.

It is this Montana that produced two of its finest artists, a painter and a writer.

Charles M. Russell painted the West. It was his subject and his inspiration. His name is linked forever with the vast herds of buffalo and cattle that he sketched on canvas. In his paintings you'll find cowboys around a campfire, an Indian on horseback braving the winter wind, a stampede of cattle or,

Laugh Kills Lonesome. *Detail of a painting by Charles M. Russell.*

On this page are two drawings by Frederic Remington. His work often dealt with western subjects.

Engravings courtesy of Colorado Historical Society

on Saturday night, of cowboys. The paintings are wonderfully realistic, filled with details of Western life, but they are also pictures of a dream. Russell gave them the romance and mystery of the West itself.

In his home, Montana, there are two galleries dedicated to the work of Charles Russell. But his paintings are also displayed in museums around the country, from the Cowboy Hall of Fame in Oklahoma City to the National Gallery of Art in Washington, D.C. They are often shown with the paintings and sculptures of another fine Western artist, Frederic Remington.

The writer, A.B. Guthrie, took his inspiration from the size of things in Montana. His great novel, *The Big Sky*, celebrates the freedom of the West. Like Russell's paintings, Guthrie's writing gives us forever a world of beauty, restlessness, freedom, and openness.

That same world has been created, again and again, in front of a movie camera. No other set-

Pictured above is writer A.B. Guthrie. His novel The Big Sky *celebrates Montana's openness.*

ting has ever so completely captured the imaginations of America's filmmakers. It seems particularly appropriate, therefore, that Montana gave the American cinema two of the brightest stars of its golden age.

He was the cowboy, forever strong, quiet, tall in the saddle. She began as the glamorous lady of films like *The Thin Man* and ended as the perfect American mother. They were both from Montana—Gary Cooper and Myrna Loy.

Above, Jack Reiner and his wife. Pictured on the right-hand page is the Prairie Symphonette.

The Prairie Symphonette

"I'm Jack Reiner and I'm a farmer and I'm also a funeral director in Scobey. I'm a cellist in this orchestra. I wouldn't be a cellist anywhere else in the world, but I can claim to be a cellist in the Prairie Symphonette."

Scobey is a town of about twelve hundred people. Not what you'd call big. And it's right out in the middle of Montana. Not exactly a suburb of New York City. It's a town where you'd probably be surprised to find a jazz quartet. And Scobey has a symphony orchestra, a symphony orchestra people go out to hear.

"People come for reasons I sometimes wonder about. If they'll clap their hands, you know, you don't really care too much about why they're doing it. You're pumped up."

Of course, the orchestra members aren't professional musicians. Like Jack Reiner, they're farmers. Like John Stenoff, they're storekeepers. Like Marlis Farver, they're nurses. Or teachers. Or clerks. But something happens when they get out there in front of people.

"You do your first public performance, and your palms are sweating, you know, and the bow is bouncing on the strings, you're so nervous. People say, 'Hey, that's okay.' And the first thing you know, you even start practicing between times."

The Prairie Symphonette obviously brings a lot of satisfaction to the people who play in it. And it seems to bring a lot of enjoyment to the people who listen to it. But why did it happen here? Why in Montana?

"This is a country of such openness, it opens the mind too. It's easy to have an accelerated imagination and vision, and that's all we're talking about here; it's just a crazy vision, you know?

Picture Perfect

In any picture of the Old West, there are vast herds of cattle grazing on the plain. In the background, there may be towering mountains against the big sky. Miles away there is a town where you can buy supplies, go to church, and have a good time on Saturday night.

That was the Old West. In some ways, it is still Montana.

There have been changes, of course. The booms and the rushes, the droughts, bank failures, oil wells, military bases, and tourists have made sure of that. Not to mention technology and just the passing of time. After all, that little town has a gas station instead of a livery stable. And there's a police department instead of a batch of vigilantes. And the editor of the town newspaper works on a computer instead of a type-

The Montana Rockies . . . as close as you can get to touching the big sky.

writer. And the schoolmarm drives a pickup. There are women running ranches and Indians providing weapons for the U.S. military. The twentieth century is alive and well in Montana.

But the cattle are still there. And the moutains. And the sky. With a little luck and a lot of care, they always will be.

Michael Reagan

Important Historical Events in Montana

8,000 B.C. Prehistoric Indians live in Montana.

1800 By this time, Plains Indian tribes—the Blackfeet, Assiniboine, Crow, Cheyenne, and Tsina—live in the grasslands west of the Rockies. Shoshone live in the southwest area.

1805 Meriwether Lewis and William Clark reach Montana.

1807 Manuel Lisa's Missouri Fur Company locates on the Yellowstone River.

1810 David Thompson maps northwestern Montana.

1852 Gold is discovered at Gold Creek.

1862 The major gold strike is made at Grasshopper Creek. The Gold Rush is on.

1863 The richest of all placer diggings is found at Alder Gulch.

1864 The Plummer gang is broken up by vigilantes. Mining strikes break out. Congress creates the Montana Territory out of a part of the Idaho Territory.

1877 The Nez Percé retreat from Idaho through Montana and are defeated in the Bear Paw Mountains.

1883 Northern Pacific Railroad enters Montana.

1884 Congress refuses to admit Montana to the Union.

1886 Terrible winter weather drives cattle raisers off the open range.

1887 The Manitoba Railroad enters Montana.

1889 Montana becomes the 41st state.

1899 Marcus Daly sells Anaconda Copper Company to Standard Oil.

1899 Supporters of Marcus Daly accuse William A. Clark of bribery and Clark is refused his seat in the U.S. Senate.

1903 Anaconda-Amalgamated declares a huge mine shutdown to break F. Augustus Heinze's control of Montana copper.

1906 Heinze sells out to Amalgamated.

1909 The Enlarged Homestead Act is passed, bringing thousands of people into the state.

1914 Montana gives women the right to vote.

1915 The copper industry is the backbone of the Montana economy. Oil drilling begins.

1916 Jeannette Rankin is the first woman ever elected to the U.S. House of Representatives.

1918 The first of a series of droughts hits Montana.

1950 The great Williston Basin opens.

1972 Montana adopts a new constitution.

Montana Almanac

Nickname. The Treasure State.

Capital. Helena.

State Bird. Western meadowlark.

State Flower. Bitterroot.

State Tree. Ponderosa Pine.

State Motto. *Oro y Plata* (Gold and Silver).

State Song. Montana.

State Abbreviations. Mont. (traditional); MT (postal).

Statehood. November 8, 1889, the 41st state.

Government. Congress: U.S. senators, 2; U.S. representatives, 2. **State Legislature:** senators, 50; representatives, 100. **Counties:** 57.

Area. 147,138 sq. mi. (381,086 sq. km.), 4th in size among the states.

Greatest Distances. north/south, 318 mi. (512 km.); east/west, 550 mi. (885 km.).

Elevation. Highest: Granite Peak, 12,799 ft. (3,901 m). **Lowest:** 1,800 ft. (549 m), Along the Kootenai River in Lincoln County.

Population. 1980 Census: 786,690 (13% increase over 1970), 44th among the states. **Density:** 5 persons per sq. mi. (2 persons per sq. km.). **Distribution:** 53% urban, 47% rural. **1970 Census:** 694,409.

Economy. Agriculture: cattle, hogs and pigs, sheep, poultry, wheat, sugar beets, barley, oats. **Manufacturing:** lumber and wood products, petroleum products, processed foods, primary metals, farm machinery. **Mining:** coal, petroleum, stone, copper, silver, natural gas, sand and gravel.

Places to Visit

Anaconda Reduction Works at Anaconda.

Giant Springs, near Great Falls.

Glacier National Park, in northwestern Montana.

Great Falls of the Missouri, near Great Falls.

Virginia City, near Dillon.

Yellowstone National Park.

Annual Events

Central Montana Winter Carnival in Lewistown (January).

Copper Cup Regatta in Polson (July).

North American Indian Days in Browning (July).

Yellowstone River Float, Livingston to Billings (July).

Midland Empire Fair and Rodeo in Billings (August).

State Fair and Rodeo in Great Falls (August).

Montana Counties

47

INDEX